We're from
Australia

Victoria Parker

Welcome
to Australia!

Heinemann Library
Chicago, Illinois

Photo research by Maria Joannou
Photography by Martin Brent
Designed by Ron Kamen and Celia Jones
Printed and bound in China by South China Printing Company

09 08 07 06 05
10 9 8 7 6 5 4 3 2 1

Library of Congress Cataloging-in-Publication Data
Parker, Victoria.
  We're from Australia / Victoria Parker.
     p. cm. -- (We're from ...)
  Includes bibliographical references and index.
  ISBN 1-4034-5782-4 (Lib. Binding-hardcover) -- ISBN 1-4034-5789-1 (pbk.) 1. Australia--Social life and customs--Juvenile literature. 2. Children--Australia--Juvenile literature. 3. Family--Australia--Juvenile literature. I. Title. II. We're from.
  DU107.P33 2005
  973'.0424--dc22

                         2004018477

Acknowledgments
The author and publisher are grateful to the following for permission to reproduce copyright material:
Martin Brent pp. 1, 5a, 5b, 6, 7, 8, 9a, 9b, 10a, 10b, 11, 12, 13a, 13b, 14, 15a, 15b, 16, 17a, 17b, 18a, 18b, 20, 21, 22, 23, 24a, 24b, 25a, 25b, 26, 27a, 27b; Corbis/Royalty Free pp. 4a. 4b. 5b. 5c. 28a. 28b. 29; Corbis/Robert Garvey p. 19.

Cover photograph of Dylan and his friends, reproduced with permission of Martin Brent. Many thanks to Carly, Georgia, Dylan and their families.

Every effort has been made to contact copyright holders of any material reproduced in this book. Any omissions will be rectified in subsequent printings if notice is given to the publisher. The paper used to print this book comes from sustainable resources.

Some words are shown in bold, **like this**. You can find out what they mean by looking in the glossary.

Contents

Where Is Australia?

To learn about Australia we meet three children who live there. Australia is a huge island. It is one of the biggest countries in the world.

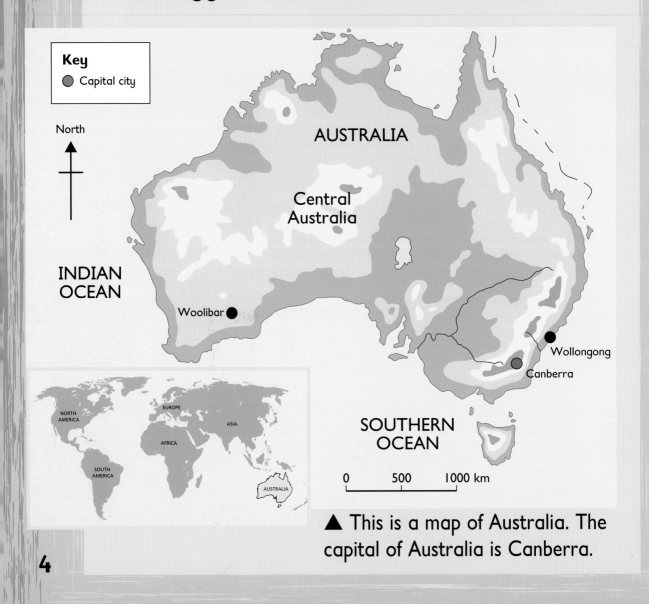

Key
- Capital city

North

AUSTRALIA

Central Australia

INDIAN OCEAN

Woolibar

Wollongong

Canberra

SOUTHERN OCEAN

0   500   1000 km

NORTH AMERICA

EUROPE

ASIA

AFRICA

SOUTH AMERICA

AUSTRALIA

▲ This is a map of Australia. The capital of Australia is Canberra.

Most of Australia is flat, hot **desert.** Many people live on the **coast,** where it is cooler. In the north, there is a large **rain forest**.

▲ Uluru is a big rock at the center of Australia.

Meet Carly

Carly is seven years old. She lives with her parents and older sister, Emma. They live in a city called Wollongong.

Carly's mother

Carly's father

Emma

Carly

▲ This is Carly and her family in front of their house.

Wollongong is on the southeastern coast of Australia. There are lots of sandy beaches there.

▲ Carly loves swimming in the sea.

At School

Carly's school is by the sea. She goes there on weekdays. School starts at 8:45 A.M. and ends at 2.45 P.M.

Hannah

▲ This is Carly and her best friend, Hannah, outside their school.

There are 32 children in Carly's class.
Their classroom is big and bright.
Carly and Hannah like learning on
the school computers.

Fun in the Sun

After school, Carly does her homework. Then, she likes to be outside. She is learning to play tennis.

On weekends, Carly spends time in the garden. Her family likes cooking on their **barbecue.** They often invite friends over.

Sports

Many Australians enjoy playing or watching sports. Carly's sister and her friends go jogging to keep healthy.

Lots of people play sports on the beach. It is fun to join a game of volleyball or to try surfing.

Meet Georgia

Georgia is ten years old. Her family runs a sheep farm in western Australia. She lives with her parents, her older sister, and the farmworkers.

Georgia's father

farmworker

Georgia's sister

Georgia's mother

Georgia

The sheep farm is on **grassland** near the **desert.** It covers a very large area. The nearest town is a long way away by car.

Down on the Farm

There are lots of jobs to do on the sheep farm. Georgia helps out. She wants to be a farmer like her parents.

▲ Georgia is helping her father fix a fence.

Georgia takes care of some of the horses on the farm. She rides a horse to help round up the sheep. Sometimes she uses a motorbike.

Living Far Away

Georgia lives too far from town to go to school. Her lessons come to her over the radio and the Internet. Once a year, Georgia goes to a camp to meet her classmates.

▲ Georgia's teacher talks to her over the radio.

Georgia's home is also a long way from a doctor or a hospital. In an emergency, the family calls the Flying Doctor.

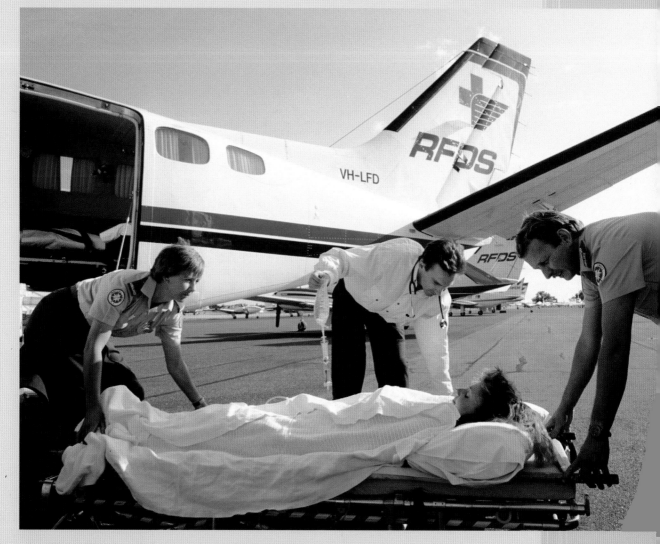

▲ The Flying Doctor comes to see Georgia's family in an airplane.

Australia's History

White people have only lived in Australia for about 250 years. People arrived from Britain first. **Settlers** from other countries made their homes there, too.

▲ This is a Turkish restaurant in the town of Alice Springs.

When white people settled in Australia, they took the land from the people who already lived there. These people are known as **Aboriginals.**

▲ Today, some Aboriginal people are being given their land back.

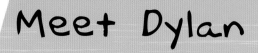

Meet Dylan

Dylan is nine years old. He lives with his mother, father, and younger sister, Natalia. His older brothers, Clifford and Dwayne, live nearby.

Dylan's father

Dwayne

Dylan

Clifford

Dylan's mother

▲ Dylan's father is the local police officer.

Dylan's family are from an **Aboriginal tribe.** They live in a **desert** town in central Australia. Dylan's home is a **bungalow** with a large garden.

At Work and Play

Dylan's school starts at 8.00 A.M. He has lessons in English, math, geography, and **Aboriginal** studies.

After school, Dylan has jobs to do. He helps by washing dishes, watering the garden, and cleaning the car. Then, he can play outside.

▲ Dylan likes going to the local pool with his friends.

Life in the Desert

The hot, red **desert** around Dylan's home is dry and dangerous. It is easy to get lost and run out of water.

▲ **Aboriginals** treat nature with great care.

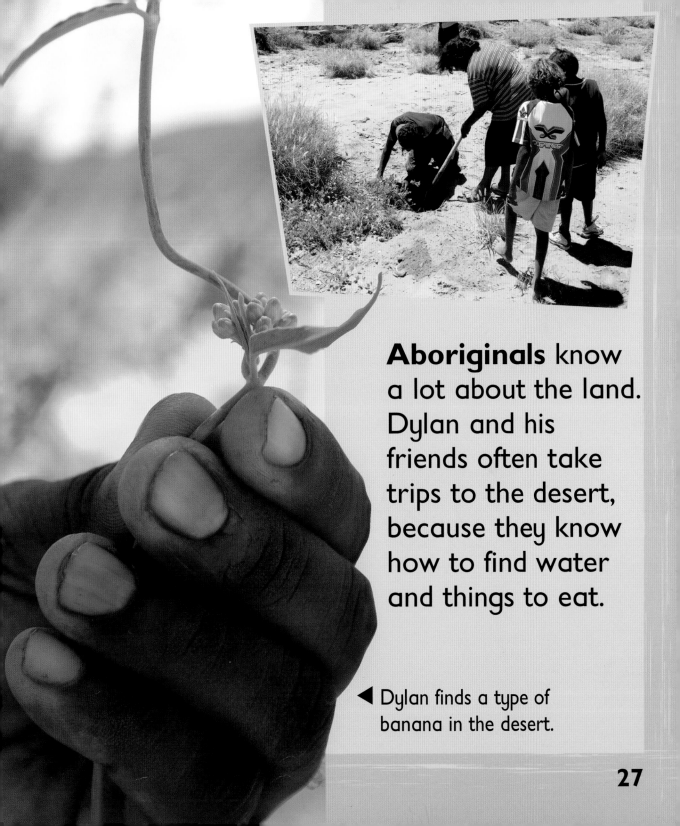

Aboriginals know a lot about the land. Dylan and his friends often take trips to the desert, because they know how to find water and things to eat.

◀ Dylan finds a type of banana in the desert.

Out and About in Australia

Australia has lots of special wildlife, such as koalas, kangaroos, and emus. There are many dangerous animals, such as crocodiles, snakes, and poisonous spiders.

The world's biggest area of **coral** is in the ocean off Australia. It is called the Great Barrier Reef. Divers go there to watch sea creatures and explore shipwrecks.

Australian Fact File

Flag

Capital City

Canberra

Money

Australian dollar

Religion
- Many white Australians are Christian. There are also Buddhists, Muslims, and Jews. **Aboriginal** Australians have their own special beliefs.

Language
- The main language used in Australia today is English. There are 20 to 50 Aboriginal languages used, too.

Try speaking Anangu Aboriginal!
These Anangu Aboriginal words are written the way they sound:

pahl-yah .... *hello, bye, good, OK*
oo-wah .... *yes*
kah-pee .... *water*

Glossary

Aboriginal people who first lived in Australia

barbecue type of grill for cooking food outside

bungalow house on just one level, without any rooms upstairs

coast where the land meets the sea

coral hard rock made of the shells of tiny dead sea creatures

desert very hot, dry area of land that has almost no rain and very few plants

grassland area of land that is mostly grass

rain forest thick forest of tall trees that grows in a hot, rainy place

settler person who comes to live in a country

tribe group of people who live closely together, sharing a language and beliefs

More books to read

Fox, Mary Virginia. *Australia and Oceania*. Chicago: Heinemann Library, 2002.

Hall, Margaret. *Around the World: Food*. Chicago: Heinemann Library, 2002.

Pyers, Greg. *Habitat Explorer: Desert Explorer*. Chicago: Raintree, 2004.

Index